THE FINALE

Calvin Miller

InterVarsity Press
Downers Grove
Illinois 60515

© 1979 by Inter-Varsity Christian Fellowship of the United States of America

All rights reserved. No part of this book may be reproduced in any form without written permission from InterVarsity Press, Downers Grove, Illinois.

InterVarsity Press is the book-publishing division of Inter-Varsity Christian Fellowship.

Distributed in Canada through InterVarsity Press, 1875 Leslie St., Unit 10, Don Mills, Ontario M3B 2M5, Canada.

ISBN 0-87784-627-8
Library of Congress Catalog Card Number: 78-70810

Printed in the United States of America

| 16 | 15 | 14 | 13 | 12 | 11 | 10 | 9 | 8 | 7 | 6 | |
| 91 | 90 | 89 | 88 | 87 | 86 | 85 | 84 | 83 | 82 | 81 |

I

When worlds cease to roll
old orbits soon become
shallow star tracks
filled with cosmic trash
and planet crumbs—the
final will and testament
of human genius.

The Singer felt a chilling wisp of air pass through the vacuum. He stood upon an asteroid and gazed upon the Center Star, still bright with fire for all its years.

Terra lumbered slowly through the radiance. She looked tired. The Singer's eyes softly saddened as he remembered her once glorious past.

He thought back on that desperate day he felt the cables on his wrists and begged the world cease its senseless murdering of love. The weary planet almost stopped, then rolled slowly on to plod the silver track before it.

"It is her final trip!" a voice behind him said.

He did not need to turn around. He knew who had followed him to his pedestal in space.

"Her very last!" agreed the Troubadour.

"Do you remember, Singer, the last day we spent together there?" World Hater asked.

"It was the day I..." He stopped and looked at his hands, "the day I knew the greatest pain of men. It is hard to call to mind that I died..."

"The day I marked your hands," the
Dark Prince finished the thought.

"Now we must go back," the Singer
said. "Terra must swelter in the
final fiery war. Her death will grieve
the Father Spirit."

"No need to grieve. Microworlds
die every day," sneered the old
antagonist.

"Yes, but dying worlds are to be
grieved, and this small mass is held
in high esteem: she is Earthmaker's
special love, and now . . ."

Again the World Hater finished the
words: " . . . and now she dies a glorious
death of hate in a bloody war that
resurrects my joy in universal bitterness.
Destruction and decay shall pave her
way to nothingness." He laughed.

The Singer spoke above his laughter:
"The time has come. What we began
before the Great Tribunal must be
resolved."

"Yes, now, out on the Plains of Man,
in the bright new capital of Ellanor."

The Dark Prince stretched his arms
outward into space. A flame exploded
on his hand. Its amber incandescence
flickered on his smirking face. "I'm
going down," he said, gesturing with
his blazing hand toward a range of
snowcapped mountains, "to the
Caverns of Death."

He rolled the flame into a sphere
between his heavy palms and hurled
it away toward Terra like a meteor. It
was all but lost to sight when it struck
the planet, lighting up the desert
where it fell.

"Ah, Troubadour, it is time for war.
At last my ancient lust for blood
shall have the banquet it desires."

He drew his cape in a great wide arc
and was gone.

The Singer gazed once more upon the
globe. Then looking starward, he
strummed his lyre and sang a requiem:

"Oh, Terra, Terra! I have
    loved you so,
And sown your golden fields
    with songs of peace.
I died to hear the music you
    should know
By now... The Song to bid your
    surging cease.

"Why, Terra, did you turn to
    hate? Infect
Your blue and earthen hope
    of joy with
Sin and greed? Earthmaker's
    love was wrecked
On your restless need for
    death and war.

"I'm coming once again through
    battlefields,
To let you know how much I
    care. I'll bear

A gentle sword whose wounds
   will heal—
Embrace you in the flaming
   carnage—share your final
   hour.

"As I once died, you too must
   pass away.
But trust my singing promise
   as your own.
My melody shall sound above
   the fray
Of battlefields: you shall
   not die alone."

He finished the requiem and turned
away, stepped off the silent asteroid
and disappeared in lingering chords
that haunted cosmic emptiness.

A passing comet swept the skyway
and hurried off in dread.

II

When the heavens finally dissolve
and the sound of splintering suns
grows deafening around colliding
worlds, some prophet will be
found extolling hope while fissures
crack the ground beneath his feet.

Beware, O earth, the prophet who
claims to know the time but
never wears a watch.

The cities stood erect. Their
windowed obelisks once were
pyramids of light. But light had
dimmed.

After ancient Urbis fell, Singerians
multiplied till every portion of their
world held shrines dedicated to the
Troubadour of Life.

Now they knew that Terra's life
imprisonment was nearly done. They
had studied THE FINALE—that book
which once had passed through the
labyrinths of lower Urbis. They
knew their empty rides around the
Center Star would soon be through.
They saw at hand the tragic, comic
ending of their world.

The War of Fire had come.

Yet war was old. It had wounded
history for centuries. Armies trained
for letting blood, and blood had
flowed from battleground to
battleground across the grieving
years. The War of Fire would be
the end of war, for when it came,
the storms of flame would reach around
the planet and set the very seas ablaze.

Men had come to know the doctrines
Everyman debated. Terra knew at
last that she was round—that all her
oceans froze in pillared ice, where
arctic seas rose up in frigid death.

Her mines contained a cold and evil
ore hidden a thousand feet beneath
the ice fields of the Crystal Range.
Brought to light the metal burst
into caustic flames that fed upon
the flesh of men. Men feared that the
ore of death would write the universal
end upon the days.

Elan, Emperor of Ellanor, owned the
mines and stored the ore in mountain
arsenals.

The upper chambers of his mines,
long since stripped of ore, were used
for other purposes. Some served as
quarters for the miners; many were
gaping caverns, eerie and empty.

Some Singerians worked in the mines
and often met to keep the Singer's
Meal and read THE FINALE, their
book of hope.

Dreamer was a miner. He had heard
the Star-Song on his journey to the
Crystal Range several years before.
Invader swirled light into his deepest
crevasses of doubt, and he was
unchained from deep servitude to
the Dark Prince. Now he drove his
mattock into the walls. He knew his
work set him against the life of
Terra, but he found refuge from his
guilt in the great Invader's light.

Dreamer suffered from a malady that
made him an uncertain resident
of two separate worlds. A queer

enchantment had first come over him
while he ate the Singer's Meal. He
dreamed of a glorious realm of life.

He loved the dream and it returned.
Gradually dream usurped reality.
He rose to levels of existence his
Singerian brothers could not
understand. The unbelieving miners
ignored his noble fantasies.

But in the dreams Invader's storms
of light obliterated all drudgery—
transporting Dreamer to walk another
world.

III

The world is poor because
her fortune is buried in the sky
and all her treasure maps
are of the earth.

Some miners near the upper shafts dressed in heavy furs to fight the frigid winds of the Crystal Range. But Dreamer dug in warmer unlit crevasses a thousand feet below. He picked the soil to find the fabled ore of death.

Dreamer's malady worsened, pushed him to the border of sanity. If he closed his eyes, the darkness of his voluntary blindness yielded light. And when the light had run its way through the chasms of his lonely spirit, it flooded past the threshold of his private world.

Dreamer finally was two men.

One kept his eyes open and chopped the death ore from its icy mountain veins. The other closed his eyes and walked a world whose glory men never had beheld. Dreamer loved the world beyond, for there he saw the only hope of life.

One night during his evening meal, he began meditating on the great Invader. Transport was immediate. Lifeland emerged. The world he loved appeared around him!

He was not alone. A hand reached out and clasped his shoulder.

He turned to see a man with royal
countenance.

"I am Ansond. Follow me and you
shall see the measure of your world.
Terra is dying. Beware Elan, and
make him not your Lord, nor wear
his sign upon your chain. Who wears
the sign of Elan bears the mark of
life in vain. For when the War of
Fire is through, Terra shall not rise
again. Come, Dreamer."

Ansond beckoned and Dreamer
moved to his command. The
Singerian's mind spun. Unbidden
flew the gleaming ground. Lifeland
rose up where majesty was found.
At the source of light rose up the
chair of sound.

A thousand, thousand towering feet
of shimmering glass—invisible,
unseen—not even there, yet standing
fast. Ansond fell on his knees and so
did Dreamer. Above them towered
the chair and a voice called out of it:
"Ansond, stand! Come forward!"

Ansond stood and saw the Singer.
Sound swirled. Trumpets lifted
up a fanfare of magnificence. Ansond
knelt before the Troubadour and
touched his forehead to the ground.

Once more he rose and faced the
Crystal Chair and cried the coronation
phrase, calling out with arms uplifted:

"Victory and power! Nobility and
honor to the Troubadour of Life!
Born from the womb of stars! King of
the Crystal Chair! Great symphony
of cosmic melodies of light! Arise
and rule till all glittering night be
born again in splendor.

"Halana to the Singer,
Earthmaker's Living Son!
Halana to the Troubadour
who reigns in sovereign song!
Halana to the planet's star!"

The Troubadour knelt before Ansond,
who took a golden vestment and
laid the rich brocade on the Singer's
shoulders. Ansond took the crown
of life and placed it on the victor's
head.

Once more he approached the Chair
of Glass and brought the Sword of
Ages to the kneeling Prince. He
offered him the hilt.

The Singer stood and raised the
blade.

Ansond and the Prince then faced
each other with their arms raised
to the glass. The Court of
Lifeland sang as one:

"Behold, the galaxy shall quake.
Starstorms will rage where dragons
    groan.
Terra bleeds upon the stake.
The Troubadour ascends the throne.
Halana."

IV

Authentic Messiahs cannot cease
their meditation on vast human hurt
   to heed the pain of nails
   in their own wrists.
Only from the cheaper, little
crosses come the cries of
impaled egoism:
   "Damnation, senseless
   killers! Oh, for a free
   hand ... and a
   machine gun!"

Ansond climbed to the pinnacle
above the Chair of Glass. He stood
and called the Phoenix down. Dreamer
strained to see the bird hovering
in the spangled canopy above the
chair. Its shrill scream pierced
the battlements:

"Beware Elan,
You sons of man!
He rides the winds
That Death transcends,
And steals all light
To rule the night
of Man!"

Dreamer awoke. Terra's dull
materiality emerged. The towering
chair dwindled to a post that steadied
him. The canopy of stars became the
gray reality of cavern walls.

Men w ₑ rushing everywhere in panic.

Suddenly he saw the reason for the
madness in the mine. From the
blackened walls there came a man,
half again as large as any miner in the
camp. He wore a chain of bronze
stars doubled at his shoulders. It
ended in a cast-iron world that bore
the name of Terra. Through the small,
iron globe a sword was run and tiny
fissures crowded out on brazen
continents and seas. His clothes were
dark, coarse and metallic, as though

they had been burnished in some
fiery war between the quarreling
asteroids. His boots were silver
corroded at the soles, for he had
waded bloody fields where Terra's
grudges grew intense from time to
time.

"I am the enemy of fire and knight
of peace," he said. "I hold the keys
that quench and yet release the
fire of Elan. I am the Prince of
Mirrors!"

Dreamer's eyes were now wide open.
No Lifeland this!

"I am the only hope for days ahead.
I've come to turn the world from war
and bless Elan's pursuit of ore that
promises to keep our planet strong
and free. Though the hour is late, the
fire is great that slumbers in these
mines. The spark that we must
quench ignites the times. I guard
and shall redeem the universe that
slumbers just above the waiting
curse."

The magnetism of his words of
warlike peace drew Dreamer. He
wanted to believe yet knew he had to
ask, "But how do you redeem?"

The giant lowered kind eyes and
extended a massive arm in warm
entreaty: "I show you now the portrait
of my hope."

He drew a silvered mirror from his
tunic and held it up to Dreamer's

face: "Here, Dreamer, is the face of
him who sets the planet free."

Dreamer stared and saw his face. His
doubts assailed the doubtful image.
The giant moved on, compelling other
miners to look into his glass. As
each in turn beheld himself, the
Prince of Mirrors cried, "You, sir . . .
and you . . . and you . . . are free with
eyes to see the only hope of man is
men."

When he had shown each one his
face, the Prince put away the glass,
and Dreamer, standing just where he
should to see the Prince's visage in the
glass, saw nothing. The angle of
reflection was correct, but the face
was not there.

The absence of the giant's face only
added to the trouble Dreamer felt
about his words. Invader stirred
within him, and he asked: "But of the
Singer? Is he not the only hope to
stay the War of Fire?"

A hardness moved across the Prince
of Mirrors as he ground out an answer
just as hard: "He is the source of
war and not the stay. Too much blood
already has been shed defending his
small peace. The times are far too
desperate for weak religion now.
It is in men that man must trust
or die."

His face grew softer as he looked upon

the simple miners and smiled at
them in joy. His love seemed pure
and warm and human.

"Men," he smiled in gifted
understanding, "you are the universal
gleam! A beacon on the polished ice
of the Crystal Mountains! You are
the light, unhideable—the hope of
Terra!"

And saying this, he turned abruptly
on his heels and walked away.

Some followed. But Dreamer stayed
to ponder why he could not see the
Prince's image in the glass.

V

"Cassandra, if the world's on fire,
We must save a cup of ashes for
   the seed."

The soldiers of the Emperor marched in rigid columns. Their era had come. The War of Fire began. Each man knew the battle plans and wore the Mark of Elan on the chain around his neck.

The tactic of their treachery was fear. At every city gate they shouted their demand that citizens within receive the Mark. If refused, they called flying Vollkons to raze the villages with fire. The Vollkons numbered only seven but the terror they inspired was beyond all measure. Terra's children sang a monstrous song:

"Seven princes on the spire,
Seven diamonds in the mire,
Seven Vollkons dropping fire
Upon the burning forests.

Who keeps the dragons in their lairs?
Elan, Lord of Ellanor."

Their rhyme was more than nonsense.

Elan kept his ugly pets in frigid eyries in the Crystal Range. Their strength demanded each be chained alone in isolated caves. Even Elan quailed before the Vollkons as a group. He knew the horror they inspired. When he unleashed them, death emerged.

The war began with what was called
the small atrocity.

One misty morning in the Season
of the Center Star, the village of
Varge was waking from the silent
night just passed. Suddenly the sky
broke clear, and through the clearing
fog came screaming Vollkons, giant
claws distended. Canisters of death
ore fell and fire was everywhere.
Children wailed and clung in flaming
death to flaming forms. All life
convulsed and died. Smoke tumbled
thick above the Steppes. Surrounding
cities saw the smoke and feared.

Word of this atrocity spread through
the Steppes. And when the smoke
cleared, Elan ordered his men into
the fear-filled world. At every city's
gate, the citizens remembered Varge
and welcomed Elan's troops. Each
was made to buy the chain of Elan and
wear the heavy medal at his throat.
Elan's bronzed medallion held but
one inscription: "Elan, Lord of
Ellanor."

On the back of every medal was a
silver mirror where each man could
behold the hope of men.

VI

Hell's logic consists in
   preventing murder by
   murdering all murderers.
Heaven's logic greets every
   murderer with grace,
   dying when the time comes
   with a beatific face.

On the evening following the passing of Varge, Dreamer finished his portion of gruel. He walked to one of the abandoned caverns to be with those Singerians who shared the drudgery of Elan's mines.

They met to sing their ancient songs and pray. But this was a special night. On the eve before, a miner had laid aside the seal of Elan and had become unchained. And on this night he waited to receive the Stigmon of the Troubadour.

While some Singerians knelt and sang the Star-Song, the miner felt the joy of wet earth in his palm. He felt a young man trace the Singer's sign upon his brow and heard him say:

"Remember as your hand is stained
That his was crushed and torn by pain
That men of Terra fully know
There is no depth he would not go
To Love.
Earthmaker, Singer and Invader be
The substance of infinity."

After the rite they read passages of hope from THE FINALE. The brazen chain of Elan slept in dust beneath their feet as they sang:

"He comes in power,
Rejoice, the hour of
    jubilee is near.
Lift up the cry
Before we die,
    our Singer will appear."

Finally, they broke the crushed
loaves and ate the Singer's Meal.
While he in reverence held his portion
of the bread, Dreamer closed his
eyes and felt awareness ebbing. He
fought, but Invader swirled in
brightness all around him, sweeping
through his hesitation. The trumpet
sounded and vivid colors blew away
the mist. He stepped back in
astonishment from the Crystal Chair.

Ansond was in armor! Its gilded
surface flashed like fire in the glassy
chair. Dreamer beheld the splendor
of Earthmaker's court of love.

Lightning struck an opaque sphere
resting in the center of the Crystal
Chair. Sound and light shot outward.

"Sorrow comes to Terra!
She wastes in furnaces
    of holocaust.
Nothing can remain.
The planet has nowhere
    now to rest but in
    the ashes of rebellion."

The Phoenix screamed above the
chair:

"Wind shall push the
    flame of war
and drive the smoke of
    suffocation through the world
Till peace has bled a
    deep immortal scar
across the hope of every nation.

Never can there come release
For Terra has despised
Earthmaker's love.
Destruction! Destruction!
The World Hater's fitful
    craze beheaded time and
    slaughtered days
Ignited truth and left the
universe ablaze."

The Phoenix flew upward, shrieking
as she fled:

"Let Lifeland know of Terra's sin,
Let the drama now begin.
Sit, Court of Evermore,
A troupe of players at the door,
Enact the drama of the end."

A trumpet sounded and act one
began.

A small blue ball rolled out in air
and a tiny world was born. Mountain
chains erupted and continents
emerged upon the sphere. Untouched
by any hand the globe revolved.
It turned slowly and unsteadily at
first. Then spun faster, then with
fury. And then it issued fire and
smoke. Then presently it flashed,

exploded into flame and disappeared.

A troupe of actors entered.

One, darkly dressed, strutted onto
the starry stage. He snapped his
fingers, holding out his hand. The
small blue ball appeared again upon
his open palm. Applause filled the
Court of the Glass Chair but the
actor sneered and snapped the fingers
of his open hand. A sword appeared
whose hilt he grasped. He raised
the sword in startling suddenness
and plunged it in the sphere. Blood
washed down the blade and drenched
his hand in red.

Horror filled the court!

"Die, Terra!" he cried out.

The other actors, stunned by this
obscenity, seemed paralyzed. The little
ball convulsed.

The evil actor gloated on the gore,
threw back his giant head and rasped
in fiendish laughter.

Ansond sensed the evil of the drama
and leapt up on the stage. The other
players fell away, and left the
swordsmen face to face.

"Give back the wounded world," the
Golden Knight cried out.

"Never!" shrieked the Black Knight.

"It is Lifeland's greatest love."

"Love cannot save it now!"

The Black Knight threw the bloody globe
into the air and swung his giant sword
completely through the wounded mass.

It split in two.

It burst in flame, and fell.

The swordsman laughed. "Love it
quickly, Ansond, for there is little
left to love."

Ansond dropped his sword and rushed
to grasp the pieces of the broken globe.
He could not let them go. He thrust
the bleeding half-worlds underneath
his cloak and smothered the flame. His
cape was fouled by smoke and blood.

He placed the broken halves together and
carried them reverently to the small
translucent plane before the Crystal
Chair.

One by one the actors lowered their
eyes and passed before the grimy
ball. They cried in one lament:

"Love is done. Hate has won.
Earthmaker's light is gone.
The Night-skies Queen is slain.
Hate has entered Lifeland and
Murdered at the throne of love."

Ansond wept and all of Lifeland with
him.

In crushing suddenness the sword
of the Black Knight pierced Ansond's
armor and sent him sprawling on the
floor.

While the Golden Knight's attention
was on the injured sphere, the
black actor had advanced and swung
his heavy blade into the golden
shoulderguards. The plate had
given way.

Ansond reeled and drew his sword.

"Come, Lord of Hate. Come to the
Blade of Truth!" He spoke to his
dark foe.

Dreamer suddenly recognized the
evil face of the Lord of Hate. The
Prince of Mirrors!

In fury then the titans met.

The lightning flashed each time the
huge swords fell. Twice Ansond fell
beneath the Black Knight's blows.
Each time he quickly rose as the
evil actor approached the small
translucent plane to abuse the
wounded world. Ansond defended it.

Gradually the black actor weakened,
and Ansond delivered a heavy
blow to his helmet. A second strike
fell soundly on the breastplate of
the Lord of Hate.

It split away.

The Black Knight cried out in his
nakedness. The other actors broke
into applause and shouts of joy.

When Ansond saw his enemy
unprotected, he drew back his blade
to plunge it in the heart of universal
hate. But the Black Knight flung
himself over the battlements and
was lost among the stars.

Ansond collapsed, fatigued in
victory. He knew the World Hater
had plunged to Terra furious in
defeat.

He knew that he must follow when
his hands were healed and his
wounded shoulder well enough to
bear the agony of battles yet to come.

The charade was nearly over and
the Phoenix came again:

"Now is the drama ended
As once it was begun.
The same hate wounds
The Golden Knight
That mauled Earthmaker's son.
Rejoice the War of Fire is won
For Terra rolls across the void
And tumbles into sun.
The Singer comes!"

The Singer came. He picked the
broken world from off the shelf and
held it high and shouted out:

"Behold, the old is gone.

The new alone remains.

"The spirit zephyrs drive a healing
    flame.
No world is ever wounded unto death.
Now shall this little globe receive
    her atmosphere,
The Father Spirit's living breath."

Incandescence flashed about his
hand. And when the light had died
away, the world was blue again.

"Terra Two!" he cried.

VII

A God too large to walk in
   human shoes
Has outgrown every hope of
   human use.
And heavy skeptics weighted down
   with doubt
Can never rise to find what
   God's about.

Dreamer found it was time to leave but feared to go where the drama was reality in process.

He took the street of monoliths that led beyond the Chair of Glass. He crossed the Azure Plain to the Final Bridge and saw the band of gray that marked the place where materiality infringed upon foreverness.

He paused and looked at the pinnacle of light. Flying from the spire a golden banner commemorated Ansond's wound and announced that the universe was now at war.

He knew that down the street of monoliths was soon to come the army Terra never could withstand.

The promise THE FINALE spoke was real. Truth would dawn upon the doubt below. The Singer was coming! The Golden Knight would not leave his side till the World Hater had been conquered. He would fight until the Emperor was vanquished and the Vollkons were slaughtered in the aerie empire of fear which they inspired.

At the entrance to the bridge he sat to stare upon the land he loved. He heard the swelling currents from

the armories of light. The knights
were lost in their own servitude
of grace. The cadence of their anthem
swelled from monolith to monolith
and rang across the Azure Plain:

"The multitudes imprisoned
    soon shall sing of
    greater light.
There are no days more
    splendid than the
    days before the end.
Whose armies can reach
    out with fire? The
    Singer's knights
Soon march with one great
    honor to defend.

He is King, He is Lord,
Singer, Prince and Troubadour."

This scene he loved but could not
stay. He closed his eyes and felt the
shock of transport. A volley of cold
air pierced his soul and he was back
on Terra.

He could hear the voice of the World
Hater preaching in another cavern.

"Man is the hope of men," the Hater
taught. "Behold hope in the glass.
I have taught this great redeeming
hope in every land, beyond the
Steppes of Varge and Thade. In a
hundred cities I have laid the final
hope of men where it belongs. Let
us wear the chain of Elan and sing

across the globe the Anthem of
the Glass."

He paused and Dreamer heard the
miners sing The Hymn of Man:

"The gods are dead, and without
    dread we cheer—
Join hands to reach and cry,
    'We shall not pass!'
We sing in confidence without
    a fear.
We wear one face, behold a
    common glass."

Above him in the upper shafts
Dreamer heard a Vollkon scream.

VIII

A humanist in choking sea
Called for help and presently
Received in full intensity
Advice.
"You must swim, if you would be.
Rescue breeds dependency;
Self-reliance makes one free."
"That's nice!"
He said,
And floated easily
And dead.

When they had finished singing,
the World Hater turned to leave,
then turned back again as if his final
words were more important than
the rest: "I go now into Terra, to
tell all of her people my good news!
I'll preach to every creature the
doctrine of the glass. Terra shall be
saved by this clear, final image of
herself."

One miner, touched by his last
words, cried out, "I too believe.
Give me the chain and glass."

As the Dark Prince handed him the
insignia, he accidentally dropped
it on the floor. As the Dark Prince
reached to pick it up, his silver cape
slid to the side, showing that his
tunic underneath was cut, the fabric
frayed. The gloomy cloth was stained
with blood. A hideous wound was
exposed—a wound that told of
conflict in the skies.

"I saw you there," cried Dreamer.
"You are the World Hater!"

"Where did you see me?" asked the
titan prince, stunned that one could
guess his great charade.

"In the other realm!" Dreamer said.

"Other realm!"

"Yes, even now you wear an injury
ill-gotten in another world."

"You have been too long in frozen
earth, poor man. There are no other
realms. You are the prisoner of time
and space like all the rest of us. Terra
is the only base of life in the lonely
sky. Men are doomed as long as they
pretend to make celestial friends.
This planet's days are done unless
men cease to speak of saints and
singers or trolls and witches in the
sky. Here, Dreamer, behold the
glass and bear our late-come hope—
the mark of peace!"

Dreamer fled in terror from the
room. His flight left those witnesses
in silent stupefaction. The only
sounds were the Black Knight's
labored breathing and the muffled,
far-off cries of Vollkons furious
in their lust for fire and flesh.

Aware they could not leave the
mines, the Prince of Mirrors yet
called out, "Go proclaim the glass
to all of Terra!"

And while he spoke he seemed to
rise and then dissolve like smoke.

Tears came into the eyes of those
beholding his illusive disappearance.
They looked at their faces in the
little mirrors on their chains and
sang again The Hymn of Man.

"The gods are dead, and without
   dread we cheer—
Join hands to reach and cry,
   'We shall not pass!'
We sing in confidence without
   a fear.
We wear one face, behold a
   common glass."

IX

A cosmic coma paralyzed
    the star.
The phantom surgeon sutured
    tenderly.
A passing comet flashed above
    the scar
And light displayed a
    planetectomy.

Across the Crystal Range the town
of Thade lay sleeping. Like Varge she
had refused the Mark of Elan and
the counsel of his peace. Her houses
were walled in stone and roofed
in slate, instead of thatch. She dared
to hope this double favor might
protect her from the fiery fate of
Varge. But flying reptiles screamed
just ahead of dawn and fire fell
everywhere.

The entire city died.

Fear stalked the living cities.
Elan won the praise of men.
Desperate children sang in terror.

"Where have the little
    cities gone?
The shadow of the
    Vollkons passed.
The flaming air denied
    the truce,
The flying dragons have
    let loose.
The very soil is poisoned
    where
The fire once hung in
    Elan's air."

Terror brought submissiveness.
The planet filled with sheep. The
armies now met frail replies and
thousands every dawn received the
chain of fear. Singerians alone

refused the glass. Many hastened
to the glistening new capital of
Ellanor, the City of Man.

Only in the center of the Empire
were they safe from Elan's fiery
wrath. Everywhere in Ellanor the
Prince of Mirrors preached the
doctrine of the glass and sang The
Hymn of Man.

Dreamer knew it was not safe to stay
within the mines. Mass arrest of all
Singerians was coming and he had
been more vocal than the rest. He
knew he had to flee the mines and
seek the enclave of the capital.

He knew he had to hurry; his
disaffection for the chain and glass
would not be tolerated long. So he
prepared to leave.

His journey would be a desperate
flight up a thousand feet of icy
shafts that passed the Vollkons'
lairs. Once outside the caves of death
the air would be so cold that even
brief exposure would be fatal. Seven
days through icy crags and narrow
ledges would he travel to the Steppes
of Varge and Thade whose ashes
inspired fear.

"Oh, Singer," prayed the Dreamer,
"May your sacrifice
Protect me from the
    Vollkons' fire
And shield me from
    the Empire's ice."

X

Evil finds a ready home
Where beauty is despised
And ugliness enthroned.

The Prince of Mirrors returned from preaching through the Empire. On every continent of Ellanor, men stood enthralled, staring at their images. "We wear one face, behold a common glass," they sang.

Elan closed all the temples to the Troubadour. He decreed that all who sang the Star-Song would be imprisoned.

Beneath the Vollkons' lairs and yet three caves above the praying miner making ready for his flight, Elan and the Prince of Mirrors met. Their covenant was brief.

"You need my doctrine," said the Prince of Mirrors.

"You need my armies more, if you would make this world you so despise sleep in terror and despair," said Elan.

"We are in league then?" the World Hater asked.

"We are. Where is your book of truth?"

"Here!" the Hater said, pulling the mirror from his pocket. "Here is the doctrine by which men most bend to our control—man's

fascination with himself. In this
small glass is subjugation so complete
it wipes away the universe. As long
as men behold themselves, they
will look no higher, my dear Elan."

"Then I pledge to our new
partnership the fire of fear," the
Emperor enjoined.

"And I . . . the image of complete
dependency—the face of man."

"I shall hold their loyalty in fear."

"I shall hold their faith in ignorance."

"Together, we control."

"Without a challenge to our
sovereignty."

"I go to burn a city."

"And I to chain man to himself."

The Black Knight tugged at his chin
until his face slipped sideways from
his head and he held his leering
visage in his hand.

The Emperor, too, began to pull his
cheek. His face split away before
his ear and then slid free.

They stood in hideous blankness,
and at length the World Hater lifted
up his face, the masque smiling
horror in his hand. Through its

open lips and eyes the room behind
was clearly visible. It leered and
spoke: "We do agree in common
hate."

"With utter lies I pledge myself,"
said the flattened face of Elan.

Then each man with his empty
hand received the other's face, and
laid it on his vacant plane of flesh
and smiled.

The faces were identical. So were
the hearts.

XI

Prayer is most real when
we refuse to say "Amen."
We most love heaven when
we will not end our
conversations quickly.
Hell is filled with those
who found their "amens"
close at hand.

While Dreamer meditated on
the perils of his flight, his aching
thoughts gave birth to drowsiness
that left him in between his two
realities. Sound shattered his
semiconscious state. The spectrum
of his mind spun, twisted into
colors swirling over gray. The
brilliance left the caverns one full
universe away.

Lifeland was thronged by a sea of
men who waited in eager expectation.
Down the Azure Plain, the Army
of the Singer moved in silence.
Dreamlike they marched in cadence
to a muted drummer who called their
steps precisely.

The Troops advanced between the
stone-faced sentries. Ansond and the
Singer led the legions. When they
arrived at the Great Chair, they
stood and reviewed the passing
troops.

The Phoenix screamed:

"Move back Galactic nebulae.
Hide the shining sea.
Make ready for the War of Wars.
Terra dies.
Leave a black place for her tomb.
Earthmaker will not stay her doom."

And then the Phoenix rose far above

her flaming column and sang the
battle hymn:

"Warfare comes to the
    Plains of Man.
Terra soon shall pass
    away.
Grandeur to the Troubadour!

Raise the praise in gilded
    flame
Till fiery letters etch the
    name
Of love across the waking
    universe.
Singer, Prince of Planets,
Troubadour of Life!"

The army raised their gleaming
halberds in the air and cried an
ancient phrase:

"Earthmaker, Singer and Invader be
The substance of infinity."

In a moment there was thunder
on the Azure Plain.

Dreamer strained to see the coming
horseman. But when the steed was
near enough to see, it rose into the
air above the plain. It soared on
graceful wings and then descended
to the Crystal Shelf before the chair.

One of the knights exclaimed, "It is
the winged Invictrix created in her
splendor to slay the Vollkons of
the Emperor."

A warrior echoed, "Earthmaker's Golden Knight shall fly and slay the seven dragons in the atmosphere of Terra."

Ansond walked to the great winged horse and placed his foot in the stirrup. He swung into the saddle.

At a single command the great steed spread her wings and lunged into the sky. The awesome span would have cast a terrifying shadow had shadows been permitted there.

XII

Come to the court of God
having eyes unwashed with
dreams and you will see
nothing.

Other hoof beats sounded in a
blinding sphere of light that came
in furious speed and thundered
to the Singer's very feet.

Dreamer closed his eyes against
the brilliance and sought to stop
his ears against the sound. A chorus
rose:

"Light-Raider comes from
    that frontier
Where stars unclustered,
    dark with fear
Cower in their eternal night
And beg Earthmaker's steed
    of light."

The light softened gradually.
Dreamer saw Light-Raider,
magnificent and opalescent. From
within his massive torso, flames
shot out in beams that swept the
court.

He had no wings yet he was larger
half again than Invictrix. His bridle
and reins were like strands of raw
color—interlaced illusions. The
saddle swam in shimmering blue-
white hues that undulated in the
towering phosphorescence of the
chair.

A small, bright object rested just
before the saddle on a little plane,

where the mane flowed round it. It
was the same blue ball the Singer
healed when the dreadful duel of
Ansond and the World Hater was
done.

Again the Phoenix flew and
interrupted Dreamer's meditation.

"Command and Dominion,
    Authority and Grace!
Earthmaker has congealed
    the emptiness of Space.
A new world comes upon
    The Singer's horse.
It is the Hour of the
    Replacement."

A hush fell over Lifeland.

The Singer walked toward Light-
Raider with deliberate steps and
as he walked he sang:

"Now is complete the Father
    Spirit's dream
Of one small planet sleeping
    in the sun
Of perfect love. The universal
    gleam
Of life as it should be is now
    begun.

Look up! Terra comes made
    new again.
A home for all of those who
    soon will be
Left planetless in space.

Poor hungry men
In sterile fields of
    inhumanity,
I take you in my injured
    hands."

While he sang he took the new world
from before the saddle and held it
high. The Court of the Chair fell
on their faces while the Troubadour
sang out his ballad to the bright
blue sphere.

"I knew your sister world.
    She flew around
Her radiant star without
    disease or pain
Or war, until the new men
    stabbed the ground
Of love. She dies and
    cannot rise again.

My Father Spirit shall not
    let her lie
A grieving vacant deadness
    in the night.
A gallant orbit shall new
    Terra fly
Where her elder sister died
    in flight.

Earthmaker's love is born
    anew
And flies the skies as
    Terra Two."

Light-Raider pawed the ground
and tossed his head and snorted.

He half-reared, then settled on his
great forelegs and knelt. The
Singer mounted. Light-Raider rose.

Taking the reins in his left hand,
the Singer raised the broad sword
in his right and led the army down
the star-swept skyway toward the
Plains of Man.

XIII

Those at Ravensbrück rejoiced
above the rumor that the
Allies were on their way.
Those about to die determined
they would live and strained
upon the housetops to catch
the first glimpse of the
color guard of freedom.

Light-Raider pranced before the host. Dreamer could see the end of ranks and files of soldiers. Some were mounted and some on foot.

He meditated on the hour when Terra One would give her orbit up and Terra Two should roll to take her place.

Whatever Elan did was now of little consequence. Whatever lies the Prince of Mirrors told, it mattered not. The Army of the Liberation was on its way.

He felt himself beginning to return and despised the steel-cold air about him. He fought but could not hold the brighter world. It slipped away. He plummeted disconsolate in gray. Terra One declared to him her morbid self.

In Dreamer's final hope of hanging on, he saw the Troubadour astride his powerful mount. With sword held high, the Singer passed the street of monoliths. The gates flung wide. Beyond the open wall a long and starless road swung down between the pale and clustered light. Even as the cavern walls closed Dreamer in, he smiled to hear the army singing through the gates:

"Raise the praise in gilded
   flame
Till fiery letters etch the
   name
Of love across the waking
   universe.
Singer, Prince of Planets,
Troubadour of Life!"

And far in advance of singing knights
the winged Invictrix flew. Above
the starless road she bore the Golden
Knight, whose wounds at last were
healed.

XIV

When comes that final frantic
    marathon
That you did not elect to run,
May there be wild flowers in
    your path,
Pray that your flight be not
    in winter, son.

Dreamer thanked Invader for his
presence. He was grateful that
his unseen friend would not abandon
him now that the hour of flight had
come.

Dreamer pulled his coat about him
and started down the passageway.
At the far end was a shaft that bore
a thousand feet of ladders in poor
repair. Dreamer's fear of the
breaches in the rungs was less
intense than his hunger to be free.

Looking up, he saw a tiny speck
of light. It was the opening above.
The laddered shaft had been a tomb
for miners who had tried escape
and failed. But youth was on his
side and his disciplined young
legs would provide strength for the
climb.

Three hundred feet above, the walls
opened outward on a cavern where
the canisters of death ore were
stacked. When he passed the arsenal,
the sentries' heads were turned
away. He moved silently on to
chambers above. Cheered by
Invader's presence, he thought
of Lifeland's army following the
winged Invictrix even now down
the skyway into Terra.

The spot of light grew larger.

He spanned a treacherous section
of broken ladder bars and passed
another room where torches burned.
Here was the chamber where Elan
and the Prince of Mirrors had lately
traded loyalty and faces.

On he climbed. The light grew. His
legs were now so weary they
trembled.

At last he came to a Vollkon's lair
and ascended through a darkened
corner of its cavern. In the flickering
torches he saw the hideous beast,
far too close at hand, feeding on
a trophy. The smell of fetid flesh was
heavy in the chamber. For a moment
Dreamer thought the Vollkon saw
him. The beast snorted, held up its
scaly head and stared at the ladder
shaft.

Dreamer's heart stopped. Two
sentries, undisturbed, dragged
up another carcass. The dragon
lowered its head and ate. Dreamer
passed on.

Above the Vollkon cavern the shaft
opened on a mountain top. Dreamer
blinked in the brilliant sunlight.
The mountains were alive with
crystalline magnificence. But
Dreamer had no time to admire the
morning. A single sentry barred
his way.

He thought he might slip quietly

behind the guard, gaining the ledges undetected. But as he stepped from the ladder points, the new snow crunched beneath his feet. The sentry wheeled. Dreamer was discovered.

The startled sentry lunged, but Dreamer stepped adroitly to the side. His assailant fell too near the opening of the shaft and only the ladder points could break his fall.

He tried in vain to grasp the wooden posts but his heavy gloves would not let his fingers grasp his hopes. He slid past the posts, clawing helplessly—first at the ladder, then at the air. His scream echoed down the cavern shafts.

Dreamer knew the wail would rouse the Vollkon feeding just below. He hurried down the sunny, icy trail along the ledges which would lead him to the Steppes of Varge and Thade.

In spite of his fatigue his legs found strength. His feet fell firmly on the snowy trail. The morning ledges were steep but comfortable. His fear of pursuit left him. The sentry lay undiscovered at the bottom of the shaft.

By afternoon the descent became treacherous. He sensed the coming of a storm. Then the trail turned upward, and he had to climb an outcropping of granite glistening with ice.

While he hung upon the wall like a frozen insect, a Vollkon scream caused his flesh to crawl. He dropped quickly upon a ledge and pulled his aching torso beneath a stony overhang.

Flattened against the wall, he watched the Vollkon pass. Its scaly wings throbbed thunder as it flew toward the Steppes of Varge and Thade. Dreamer's fear was intense but groundless. The Vollkon was not seeking him.

Only when the dragon passed could he notice that two men rode the saddle on its neck. He could not see their faces but the second wore a black cape that fluttered in the air and the fabric underneath the fluttering cloak was frayed.

XV

Conflict is the habit of the ages.
War's amputees sire children eager
to mature and take their bloody
turn at death.

Sir," a sentry said, "there are
reports an army is advancing toward
the Plains of Man."

"From where?... What cities?"
Elan asked.

"From none we know," the guard
replied.

"By horse or foot?"

"Both. Horsemen first, followed
by an infantry of magnitude."

"Then send the Vollkons. We'll set
the cities blazing in their path. The
fire will turn the rebels back."

"They are said to be a buoyant
army," the sentry offered.

"Buoyant?" Elan seemed puzzled.

"Buoyant!" the sentry repeated.
"They sing as they march."

"What about their marching makes
them sing?"

"The words, sir, have to do with
the crowning of some singer as their
universal king."

"The Singer!" cried Elan. "We
sealed his gilded temples!"

"We have. Many have been burned."

"And still his superstition lives,"
said Elan in disbelief.

"They sing of him ... this army.
A general leads them. His horse is
said to be so white that he appears to
be illuminated from within."

"Send the Vollkons! Burn cities
in their path!"

The courier left. From high in the
Crystal Range the Vollkons flew.
East of the Plains of Man twenty
cities burned. Elan was sure the
burning cities would repel the
rebel horde, if such a horde existed.

The Prince of Mirrors was undaunted
by rumors of a coming war. He
preached his doctrine of the glass
in the capital as he had preached
it throughout the troubled provinces.
By now the insignia and seal were
everywhere. Invader forbade
Singerians to accept or wear the
chain. Their disdain of mirrors and
the Prince was widely known.

So persecution came. Those who
refused the mirror and the seal
were put in prison. When Singerians
could obtain bread from the prison
larders, they crushed the loaves
and ate the Singer's Meal. Beyond
the prison walls men smashed
mirrors and laid by the seal of Elan.

Each month thousands cried out to
be unchained and received the
Stigmon as Terra's men had done in
every generation. The prisons
quickly filled and overflowed to
improvised detention centers and
temporary workhouses.

Elan began a curious plan. The
temples of the Troubadour were
many, for Singerians had thrived in
freer days. Elan ordered the gilded
temples converted into prisons:
windows were barred and doors
were bolted. Singerians were
imprisoned where once they were
most free.

Their liberation, Elan said, would
be an easy matter. They had only
to take the chain and publicly profess
the doctrine of the glass.

"Do you believe the Singer lives
on?" said Elan to the Prince of
Mirrors.

"He never lived," the World Hater
replied.

"Yet they say he's coming down some
magic skyway and soon sets foot on
Terra."

"It is the hopeless tale of the
oppressed. Every desperate age
invents messiahs," said the Prince.

"But, were it true..." Elan hesitated.

"Were the Troubadour alive and
general of an alien horde, could he
be stopped with Vollkons or with
armies?"

"I can't say. Men have talked for
centuries about a War of Fire. The
old Singerians have it written in a
book called THE FINALE. But why be
troubled? If the Singer stood now
upon the Plains of Man, would you
surrender or fight?"

"I'd fight!" shouted Elan. "I'd
give him such a thrashing in the
flames . . ."

"Then I cannot see that it matters
if the rumor's true or not."

"I've burned a score of cities already.
I think it is an idle tale . . . Still,
thousands have perished to show
him my force, should it indeed
be him who leads this fabled host."

They walked together as they talked
and soon were along the balustrade
above the royal residence.

"Are you afraid, Elan?" the Prince
of Mirrors asked.

"No! Still I must go to the
Plains of Man and see if this army
exists."

A Vollkon winged above the city.
Its ugly head dipped low above

the royal buildings. Its teeth
were parted. The scaly plates of its
abdomen were like corroded brass.
Its six deadly claws were ready
for the bidding of its Lord. Its six
wings brought a turbulence like
thunder.

It came to rest upon a marble finial
and became a gargoyle on the palace
wall grinning at the people far below.

Elan beckoned. The reptile left its
perch and flew to him. He placed
his foot upon a heavy wing and
climbed across the dorsal scales.
He sat down in the saddle on the
grotesque neck. The dragon moved
into the air and soared above the
smoke of twenty cities.

XVI

"Good-bye, cruel world!" his
letter said pinned to his shirt above
the red. His world was cruel. We
wondered why he felt he had
to say "Good-bye!"

Dreamer shivered in the cold. The
moon was bright and he decided to
move rather than sleep in snow
and ice. He knew the Troubadour
was either on the skyway or this very
planet where he trembled in the
cold.

The trail turned down again.
The frozen air stung his face.

By dawn of the second day he knew
he had to rest. Desire had driven
him to fatigue that could no
longer be ignored. The Steppes
were still three days away. But the
worst part of the trip was behind.
The slopes became gentle, the cold
less severe.

He rested in a sunny place. There
was no wind. The morning sun felt
warm. He slept without awareness
of the altitude and cold. His sleep
erupted suddenly in cyclone colors.
The streets of Lifeland were empty.
While his weary flesh slumbered
on the trail, he ran down the Avenue
of Obelisques across the Phoenix's
Court. The gates were open, and the
Army of the Liberation was so far
down the skyway they could not be
seen.

Dreamer was ecstatic! The Singer
might be on the Plains of Man.

A new excitement claimed him. The
invasion might come while he slept
upon the trail.

There was little point in staying
longer. Lifeland did not exist without
the Singer. Dreamer did not rest. He
opened his eyes, stood, then hurried
forward into afternoon.

At sunrise of the third day, he lay
and slept as Invader stirred within.
Sleep had lost desire and would
not transport him to empty streets.

But he had a different kind of dream.
He dreamed of a stable where a black
horse stood waiting while a man in
black clothes ground his sword upon
an emery wheel. The sparks flew in
Dreamer's mind. He recognized the
titan knight who toiled at the
wheel as the Prince of Mirrors.
Dreamer knew that the crude stable
would be his first stop in the capital
of Ellanor, though he knew not
why. Nor was he sure why Invader
showed him this, but he trusted
inner light.

When he awoke, his feet sped with
lightness, as did the days upon the
lower ledges of his flight. Finally,
he came to the Steppes of Varge and
Thade. They had been the first
to suffer in the War of Fire. Now
twenty other cities to the east were
smouldering in death. When Dreamer

saw the carnage, he wept.

Varge and Thade were dead. Whole
cities gone! Only ashes where once
the children played and sang their
rhymes:

"Seven princes on the spire,
Seven diamonds in the mire,
Seven Vollkons dropping fire
On the burning forests.

Who keeps the dragons in their lairs?
Elan, Lord of Ellanor."

"It is a mad existence," Dreamer
thought, "when nonsense rhymes
contain the only sense there is."

He was about to proclaim all life
meaningless, when Invader stirred
him to remember: the Singer was
the only value in a senseless
universe.

Against the morning sun, above the
smoking ruin, rose up the glistening
towers of Ellanor.

XVII

Death is a confirmation of
   the believer's creed.
For the skeptic it is discovery,
   immense and late.

Elan soared above the smoking
cities. Nothing stirred. Death was
universal. He gloated on his power.
The rumor of the alien army was a
farce. Beyond the devastated,
blackened earth he saw nothing.

And then his blood ran cold! In the
sky ahead—in the sky, where only
Vollkons rode—he saw a great
winged horse bearing a man in
armor. Beneath the flying cavalier
he saw the army. For the first time
in his reign of tyranny, Elan doubted
Elan. He drew the reins on his
dragon's head and the reptile turned
back across the burning ash toward
the Plains of Man.

He knew his fires had been in vain.
Burning cities would not stop these
aliens. He pondered their origin
and feared the flying horse. He
remembered old tales that spoke of
days of doom and wars of fire.

His bravado ebbed. Was he Emperor?
Did he have Vollkons? Was his city
safe?

He smiled upon his former fears,
then glanced back. The sun on
Ansond's golden armor nearly
blinded him. He heard the singing
host:

"Raise the praise in gilded
  flame
Till fiery letters etch the
  name
Of love across the waking
  universe.
Singer, Prince of Planets,
Troubadour of Life!"

His Vollkon screamed. And—for
the moment—its piercing cry
blotted out the battle hymn below.

XVIII

To break a mirror always brings
seven years of evil luck,
Unless you have run out of years.

The World Hater knew that Elan had
discovered the invasion. The day
the Hater had long anticipated could
no longer be forestalled. The wound
in his shoulder had not healed,
and the fight would come before it
could.

He hurried through the back streets
to the stable where his horse and
armor waited.

He took a large sword hanging
there and placed the edge against
the emery stone. He pumped the
treadle and the stone revolved.
The steel bled sparks.

His great black horse tossed his
head and snorted. He was ready for
the contest that his master would
soon begin. The Prince of Mirrors
hated Terra and would be glad
to see it burn. Still he wondered
where he would go when the object
of his hate had perished in the
crematorium of war.

He turned the other edge of the
blade upon the wheel. Again blue
sparks leaped into the dark.

The door burst open and the fugitive
Dreamer beheld the Prince's work.

"Can this be? The Prince of Mirrors

preaches peace and sharpens swords!
You cannot win! I left Lifeland six
days ago. Ansond's wounds have
healed and your torn flesh still
gapes. The battle you began with
Ansond you must finish with the
Troubadour himself, World Hater!"

"Why must you use my former
name?" the Prince of Mirrors said.

"It is the only name you ever really
had."

"I'll kill you, Dreamer, and the
world will bless me for your
execution," the Hater spoke with
force.

"Will not Terra think it odd that
he who preaches peace kills those
who disobey the doctrine of the
glass?"

"Look!" the Dark Prince cried.
"Come wear the chain and seal.
Look..." he repeated pulling a
mirror from his tunic. "In this glass
lies the hope. Behold your face and
live."

Dreamer tore the mirror from the
titan hand and the giant could
not stay his force. The Hater quickly
grasped the sword and sent it singing
through the air.

"Lower, and you may take my head,"
shouted Dreamer, "but you would

only have it till the morrow. For then death itself will be forever dead, and your spell of terror will be done."

Dreamer felt the inner courage of the great Invader. "Beware, World Hater. I have seen your adversary and he is mighty. And your poor horse cannot withstand Light-Raider. The War of Fire has come. Tomorrow you begin a kind of dying never to be dead. It is your final day to make this world afraid. It is this world's last night. You cannot win!"

"I beat him once upon the wall!" screamed the World Hater.

"Another lie to fit another face! You were beaten then just as you were beaten in the Court of Lifeland. You wear the festered wound. Tomorrow you will lose the third and final time."

The Dark Prince hated him for knowing of his defeats. His face contorted with the hatred he had masked so well in messages of love and peace. The sword blade flashed in the lantern fire.

Dreamer dodged and flung the mirror. It struck the giant in the chest, toppled to the floor and shattered. Dreamer fled into the night.

"He's coming, tomorrow!" he
shouted back into the stable.

The World Hater ground his teeth
and threw down his sword in
senseless anger. It fell into straw.
He winced at the pain in his shoulder
where the wound still seeped upon
his cloak.

Why would the ancient wound not
heal?

XIX

The first sound sleep we ever get
   on earth
We must be roused one realm away.

The Royal Road to the City of Man ran through death. The Singer wept as he beheld the charred etchings of city skylines. Nothing lived. The Army of the Liberation rode in silence.

At length, the Singer drew Light-Raider's reins and slid from the saddle. Terra Two rested firm upon the saddle shelf, even as the grand horse threw his head toward the sky when the Troubadour dismounted. He led his horse through the carnage of Elan's infamy.

As his boots moved through ashes that had once been the city of Aishorihm, his foot fell against an object in the swirling ash. Around the wasted torso of a decaying corpse was the seal of Ellanor. The tiny mirror reflected only ash.

Aishorihm had died for him who wished to rule the universe in his own name. The soldiers closed ranks silently behind the Troubadour. Their faces glistened as their eyes beheld the charred remains of depravity on Terra.

When he had walked and wept, the Singer mounted once again. In somber tones he sang above the

ash of Aishorihm those haunting
words that he had sung so long ago:

"They died absurdly whimpering
    for life.
They probed their sin for
    rationality.
Self murdered self in endless
    hopeless strife
And holiness slept with
    indecency.

All birth was but the prelude
    unto death
And every cradle swung above
    a grave.
The Sun made weary trips
    from east to west,
Time found no shore, and
    culture screamed and raved.

The world in peaceless orbits,
    sped along
And waited for the Singer
    and his song."

The Singer sang no more. The smoke
was too intense, his tears too
frequent.

By noon they passed the zone of
ashes and moved on toward the
capital of Ellanor.

In an instant Ansond soared low
above the troops and cried,
"Vollkons!" He then flew on ahead.
The army halted and watched the
skies.

The evil shadows passed at
stupefying speed. Then fire was
everywhere! The flame scorched
the earth about their feet, then
fled. It blazed on each knight's
armor and yet it did not burn.

The army cheered and soon paid
little heed to falling fire. Their
eyes were turned to the skies, where
Ansond and Invictrix sped to halt
the flying dragons.

Ansond drew his sword to face
the largest Vollkon. Invictrix
maneuvered quickly and in the
first pass Ansond's blade cut one
talon from the beast. The severed
claw, still grasping its canister
of death, impacted on the ground
and scattered flame.

The wounded Vollkon lunged
forward. Invictrix flew at angles
till the sword of Ansond was beneath
the Vollkon's scaly abdomen. He
drove his giant blade between the
armored plates. The dragon's blood
rained down upon the field below,
and then the dying reptile plunged
into the fire storm it had created.

Ansond felt a crushing jolt. The
huge talons of a second beast lifted
him to stare upon its ugly head.
A shaft of pain shot through him
where the dragon grasped his
shoulder. The gaping jaws were
open to devour him. As he passed

the giant eye, he plunged his sword
into the mirrored surface. The eye
split open. The Vollkon screamed
and dropped the Golden Knight.
Invictrix broke his fall by flying
underneath him in midair.

The Vollkon writhed as once again
Ansond drove his sword between
the armored underplates. The second
shrieking beast fell to the fiery
earth.

Two Vollkons yet remained. One,
sensing danger, flew away but
Invictrix overtook it, preventing
its escape. The Vollkon, still
carrying one canister of ore, hurled
it against the harness of the flying
horse. A fiery sphere engulfed
both steed and rider. The light
paralyzed the knight for a moment,
and again the Vollkon tried escape.
Then the globe of flame shattered
as Invictrix bounded into clear sky.

In a spectacular maneuver Ansond
leapt from Invictrix and dropped
astride the back plates of the dragon.
The beating of the scaly leather
wings was deafening. Yet no matter
how the Vollkon tried, it could
not wrench the knight from its
back.

Ansond poised his sword at what
appeared to be a set of shoulder
blades. He plunged the blade
between them and the dragon

screamed and died aloft. Ansond
leaped into the air and once
more alighted in the saddle of his
steed.

The final beast, bewildered by
the rapid death of the others,
prepared to throw its last remaining
charge of ore. Ansond flew directly
at its face and swung his sword
down through the canister the
Vollkon held. It exploded and the
searing flash enveloped both knight
and dragon. Invictrix passed unhurt
through the bright circumference
of fire. But the reptile fell, its
burning hulk colliding hard with
earth.

The Army of the Liberation still in
battle columns cheered and sang:

"Then came Ansond in skies
   filled with fire
And faced the great dragons
   of hate.
In the fiery world where the
   battle unfurled
Their flight came too little
   and late.

"Ansond the Golden has brandished
   his light
And the beasts of war have not
   fled.
Fire burns on his sword and the
   Black Knight
Shall die where his dragons
   have bled."

And then they sang the magnificent
hymn of the hosts:

"Warfare comes to the
    Plains of Man.
Terra soon shall pass
    away.
Grandeur to the Troubadour!

"Raise the praise in gilded
    flame
Till fiery letters etch the
    name
Of love across the waking
    universe.
Singer, Prince of Planets,
Troubadour of Life!"

XX

"The sky is falling!"
said Henny Penny.
"No, poor bird, it
only seems that way
when the earth is
rising to higher
levels of righteousness
and love."

Elan could not believe it. Four
Vollkons had perished in the
encounter. In the days that remained
he had to mobilize his legions.
They were at battle stations on the
Plains of Man, facing the east in
numbers so abundant that their
armor seemed a silver ribbon around
the walls. Alert, the soldiers waited
and watched the road to catch sight
of the alien horde. They scanned
the skies to catch a glimpse of
Ansond's horse. But the bleak day
ended and nothing yet was visible.

The three remaining Vollkons had
been busy carrying the canisters
of ore from the Crystal Range to
the central armory well inside the
City of Man. It was clear to Elan
that the capital was the destination
of the Singer's troops and the likely
site of conflict. When all the ore
had been transported, the Vollkons
perched on the eastern wall above
the troops of Ellanor like a crown
of evil on a doomed city.

Fear gnawed the capital. The city
had been sealed. The gates were
bolted and the drawbridge drawn.

Inside the city those who wore the
chain and seal heard rumors that an
alien army stretched around the
planet.

Who were they? Where was their
kingdom? Who were the flying
knight and singing general? And
most plaguing of all, "Why could
Vollkons not destroy them?"

The Singerians inside the city
were jubilant. "He comes!" they
said as they met each other in the
dismal streets.

At the beginning of the second day,
while the soldiers gathered in
formation on the plains, the Prince
of Mirrors rode through the streets.
For the first time he was on his
horse. He wore a helm, breastplate
and sword. His eyes searched every
crowd he met. He sought but could
not find Dreamer. The Death Stallion,
a black steed who matched the
giant's hulk, was ominous.

"Dreamer is in the city," the
Prince of Mirrors said to Elan, who
showed small concern. "Elan! He has
escaped your mine in the Crystal
Mountains and has crossed the
Steppes of Varge and Thade on foot.
He is here now in the capital telling
everyone of the military exploits
of the Singer and his knights. He
is preaching in the streets that
Ellanor will perish in the War of
Fire. He dismays those who wear
the seal and chain. He cries that
all must now repudiate the doctrine
of the glass."

Elan sensed the fury in the voice.

"His bleak words," continued the
Black Knight, "set the city in dismal
doubt about your ability to defend
it. Let us now impound all Singerians
not already in our prisons and put
them to death!"

"It is the only way," agreed Elan,
somewhat absently.

"Now!" demanded the Dark Prince.

"Yes, now. There is very little time,"
Elan said.

The Prince of Mirrors rode to the
armory and made the announcement.
The sentries arrested everyone
who did not wear the chain.
Singerians were ferreted from homes
and alleyways, and placed in an
old building near the armory.

The Prince of Mirrors watched
the arrests but still did not see
Dreamer. When all had been
collected, the Hater rode his horse
through the guarded doorway of the
temporary compound. When they
saw him in their midst, the
Singerians began to chant, "He
comes! He comes! He comes!..."
Their voices grew in volume till
the Black Prince could not stand
the roar.

Then they began the chorus:

"The Prince of Dragons
  soon must fall
Before the Prince of
  Planets."

The World Hater had no tolerance
for their music. He had heard it
through too many centuries. He
once had hoped to grind the music
into silence. Now the hour was late
and the music rose around him
with foreboding. The Death Stallion
pranced uneasily amid the mob.

The Prince of Mirrors reined the
horse so sharply that it reared into
the air and wheeled upon its
haunches. He swung his long sword
in each direction and the hooves
of his steed fell again and again.
The brandished blade cut
indiscriminately. Then quickly
he departed.

Dreamer had been arrested with
the others. Yet he had not been
discovered by the Dark Prince.
From the shadows of the makeshift
prison he beheld the massacre and
wept. He embraced an old and dying
woman, careless of the gore clotted
on her wrinkled face.

"He comes!" he said to her.

"He comes!" she said through
pain. Her smile froze into silence.

The Invader swirled hope through

the darkened room like hurricanes
of light. His brilliance pushed
back the gloom. Joy washed down
their faces. "He comes!" they cried.

The dead were moved to the center
of the room as the Singerians
voiced the words of THE FINALE they
had left too long unsung:

"He comes in power,
Rejoice, the hour of
    jubilee is near.
Lift up the cry
Before we die,
    our Singer will appear."

XXI

Take your visions.

Give me photographs.

The book of visions always has
blank pages, for the mystics
never can agree on exactly
what they saw.

The album's filled with photographs
where lens and light and silver
nitrate record the moments as
they were.

A steady light may be observed.

A flash, however brilliant, is
debated.

Three hours before the dawn, the stone face of the prison house crumbled. The roof blew away. The prisoners stood at once to their feet. Through the devastated walls they saw the starry sky. One star began to grow, flooding the sleeping city with its light. It settled ever closer until it came into their very midst.

"He is here!" shouted Dreamer.

The glare softened into friendly incandescence and then into a glow.

Invader had gathered the harsh light around him and swirled it ever faster until the two great lights converged in a blinding supernova, then softened once again.

A great horse emerged from the brilliance and the Troubadour dismounted.

The prisoners fell upon their faces.

The Singer with one hand held Light-Raider's reins and with the other palm he lifted up the face of a young man.

"It is over," he smiled. "I have come!"

The lad leapt upright and embraced
the Troubadour. The Singer threw
his arms around the youth and kissed
him.

An older child ran to embrace the
pair.

At once the assemblage converged
upon the trio. Their joy was
immense.

Dreamer had never been so happy.

The long-awaited Prince had come!
Then Dreamer saw the woman who
had died in his arms. She was alive
and reaching to the Troubadour. So
were all who had been slain. The
Singer knew the old woman as he
knew them all. He walked to her.

"Will I ever have to die again? . . . It
was so . . . so . . ."

"I know how it is to die," he smiled.
"But dying is over now."

"Come with me," the Singer called
out to the other prisoners. They
followed him outside. The sentries
looked yet never saw them. Light-
Raider and the Singer led them
through the streets. Invader's light
moved ahead of them. The streets
were swelled with people from each
quarter of the city. Singerians
came—smiling, running, dancing
through the gates.

There were many in the streets
and yet the army of Ellanor did not
rise to quell the unseen midnight
riot.

Near the gates, the Troubadour
swung back into his saddle. Invader's
light glinted from his crown and
he raised his swordpoint to the city
gates.

The gates opened and the drawbridge
lowered itself across the moat.

The liberated prisoners sang
boldly and advanced through the
gates. Even as they passed Elan's
troops, they sang without fear. The
sleeping Vollkons never noticed
them or heard their songs:

"The Golden Age has dawned
    upon the grave of time
And we are free!
We lay aside the chains of
    our humanity.
The Singer comes to save the
    remnant of the age.
The gates fling wide!
The banner waves above the
    Troubadour of Life
Astride a steed of light!

"He comes! He comes!
The blind can see!
The halt march perfectly!
The prisoners are free!

"He comes! He comes! He comes!
Lift his name, his universal
    love.
Spread majesty in light above
    the stars,
For we are free!"

The Army of Liberation heard the
captives singing and the soldiers
erupted in an anthem of their own.

The realms met.

Lifeland and Terra at last were one!

In the daisied meadow soon to be
a blazing field of war the liberators
and the liberated sang as one:

"Raise the praise in gilded
    flame
Till fiery letters etch the
    name
Of love across the waking
    universe.
Singer, Prince of Planets,
Troubadour of Life!"

And the spectacle of life began.

The Army of Liberation fell upon
their faces as the Troubadour
approached. The liberated captives,
too, bowed themselves to the ground.

The Singer sat resplendent on his
horse and looked upon the union
of the ages.

He lifted up his glittering sword
to the great glass chair so many
light years distant:

"Father Spirit," he cried
    into the night sky.
"It is done. They are yours,
Earthmaker, the Magnificent!
These are the evidence that
    only faith is sane,
And never more shall freedom
    wear a chain.
Hate is vanquished. Joy has
    won!
Now ends the flight of
    Terra One.
And Terra Two shall fly the
    newer sky
In love."

While every knight knelt, Terra
Two rose gently in the air from the
shelf before the saddle.

There boomed above the plain a
gallant chorus rising somewhere
deep in space. It was an old, old
song and the tune reached hauntingly
again to touch the Father's face.

And Terra Two began to grow. It
spun in midair, rose high above
Light-Raider as the Star-Song echoed
through galaxies.

"The melody fell upward
    into joy
And climbed its way

in spangled rhapsody.
Earthmaker's infant stars
   adored his boy,
And blazed his name in every
   galaxy.''

The plains of Ellanor were suddenly
baptized in a golden incandescence,
nearly as luminous as that which
lit the Azure Plain of Lifeland.
Each of the newly liberated fell in
double columns that flanked a
blinding aisle down which the Singer
passed. Dreamer found himself in
the long column on the right.

He waited till the Troubadour passed
in front of him. Like others who
preceded him in the column, he
knelt. The great sword touched his
shoulders, and the cool blade on his
naked flesh was the confirmation
that he was now part of the Army
of Liberation.

When the Singer had passed,
Dreamer stood with the firmness
of a victor. He stiffened with
military air when he realized he was
dressed like all the other soldiers.
The silver mail hung upon his arms
and shoulders. The Symbol of the
Singer was raised in bronze relief
above his breastplate. His sword
lay flat within the scabbard that
rested against the greaves, and his
gauntlets were tucked behind his
studded belt.

What had happened to the woolen
rags he had worn only moments
before? He didn't know, but he wore
the new dignity well. He knew that
tomorrow he would fight the War
of Fire. His hand rested firm upon
his sword and he smiled.

XXII

Light is never given
while we fear the dark.

When dawn came, the Army of
Liberation drew their swords and
began the advance. They marched
in silence toward the enemy columns
stationed by the wall. Elan, in the
saddle of a Vollkon laden with
the ore of death, advanced to meet
the enemy. His bridled reptile
released the canisters. Fire fell
everywhere, but the Army of
Liberation marched on.

Elan feared.

The unbridled Vollkons flew again
to the armory and returned to hurl
more fire. The heat grew so intense
that the forests near the Plains
of Man ignited. Sheets of flame
swept in waves across the land
and licked the base of the fortress
walls. It looked as if the entire
globe would burn.

Elan made a tactical error. He
decided that the Singer must be
killed to stop the onslaught.

Astride his great dragon Elan dived
toward Light-Raider who did not
bolt.

Giant claws grasped for the
Troubadour but could not sweep
him from his horse.

Then suddenly the Vollkon looked
toward the sky and screamed.
Ansond closed on him. The Golden
Knight recalled a ploy he had
used in earlier attacks and sliced
through the canister which Elan's
dragon grasped. Fire engulfed both
beast and rider.

As the saddle girth collapsed and
the searing flame rushed over him,
Elan wailed in terror. In separate
moments yet almost one, Emperor
and Vollkon hit the earth.

Two Vollkons remained. One
wheeled and confronted winged
Invictrix in the air. Wildly its six
great talons ripped the air. Invictrix
barely kept beyond the reach of all
its savage claws. Each way the horse
flew, the beast turned in the air to
face Ansond and fight. The roaring
Vollkon almost deafened those
below. The reptile opened its deadly
jaws to grasp the horse's wings.

Below the screaming skies, the battle
ranks began to close. Along a
hundred-mile front, sword clashed
on shield. The wail of dying men
continued through the day. Above
the din of war echoed the cries of
dragons in the air.

By afternoon the Vollkon had
begun to tire. Invictrix circled it
until the sun fell full into the
monster's face. The reptile's glazed

eyes spoke its death ahead of time.
Its wing beats slowed and finally it
settled toward the earth. It could
not rise although it longed to do so.

Invictrix and her rider watched
the beast descend. It hovered for
a moment above the thickest combat,
then fell the few remaining feet.

The men of Ellanor moved back to
give the dragon dying space. Its
great leather wings fluttered like
a crippled gull. Its claws dug into
the bloody earth among the corpses
of the fallen soldiers. It whimpered,
groaned and gasped. Then died.

The dragon's slow, painful death
unnerved the men of Ellanor. They
had reason to fear. Elan was dead.
Terra was aflame and the fire had
spread to the capital. The gates
were now ablaze.

Ansond turned to the final Vollkon.
The beast, knowing it was the last,
had lost its heart for war. It would
not fly. It perched like a great stone
gargoyle on the palace armory
where the canisters of death ore
were stacked in pyramids.

As Invictrix flew close, the Vollkon
toppled backward, scattering the
deadly piles.

It could not fold its wings. Spasms
shook its ugly head. Froth

poured above its forked tongue.

Seized by desire to end its existence,
it brought a merciful conclusion
to the war. Grasping a canister, the
Vollkon tore the frail shell until
it burst. In an instant fire shot high.
The whole armory detonated. Flame,
growing in intensity, collected in
a golden ball and settled on the city.

Terra was ablaze! Hate's final grudge
against Earthmaker's love was
holocaust.

Dreamer, turned Avenger, struggled
to find the Prince of Mirrors in the
burning city. He was confused by
all the flame. The streets were filled
with the fallen, and the buildings
were in ruins. He sought the stable
where the Dark Prince had sharpened
his weapon for the conflict.

A cloud of dense smoke blew across
the small lane where Dreamer
walked. A burning timber crashed
ahead of him and exploded in a
shower of sparks whose light was
smothered by the soot and darkness.

He fought the smoke and, shielding
his face against the heat, he stumbled
through the hot mist. When Dreamer
drew his arm back to breathe, the
Prince of Mirrors stood directly
in the burning way.

The Hater grinned and drew his sword.

XXIII

Materiality: A blessing all its own.
Spirit-Demons play in fire
hoping for cremation.
In the terror of their immortality
they envy dying men.

In the days prior to the Liberation, Dreamer would have been terrified by the leering Hater. Now he was amazed that the aggressor's grin left him unafraid. The Hater's sword was twice the size of his, but he drew his own blade and stepped the thirsty distance to his foe. The Hater swung. Then the smaller swordsman hurled his steel in a direct arc that would have hit the Hater's armor. The sound of clanging steel resounded through the streets. Each stalked the other. Again their blades resounded as Dreamer slowly weakened.

Suddenly Ansond bolted through the smoke, calling to the Hater, "Come! Leave the Dreamer! Your wounded shoulder still seeps my grudge."

"Not before I finish with this miner," the Prince of Mirrors cried. He followed his defiance with a question, "Is Elan dead?"

"The planet's dead!" cried Ansond, "and Elan with it. He fell in flame from a slaughtered Vollkon."

"He died wearing my face," mused the World Hater, ". . . but no matter, I have his."

"Terra died because it wore your
face," Ansond interrupted.

Gesturing to the flames the Hater
cried, "Look, Ansond! I have laid to
rest Earthmaker's hope and smashed
his finest work of art. Behold the
power of hate!" He laughed.

Dreamer watched the unfolding
conflict. Suddenly he was dazzled
by blinding intensity. Light-Raider
bolted through the wall of flame.
Ashes formed whirlwinds beneath
his hooves. The Singer came.

"It is your final moment!" called
the Singer.

"Perhaps," the Dark Prince said.
"The planet burns and the flames
spread. Perhaps the seas themselves
shall erupt in flame," he laughed.

"Indeed they will," the Troubadour
agreed. "Hate sometimes has a
fiery end before it is absorbed in
love."

The old antagonists faced each
other as the Troubadour continued.
"My Father-Spirit loved this place
and the men he made to live here.
"Now . . ." He seemed choked by the
declaration. "Now . . . both his
world and men are gone."

"I told you I would win," sneered
the World Hater. "I warned you

at the wall. The fight was fair. Now
see the ash can of your artistry."

"You have not won ... Look!"
Ansond sent his mount through
the wall of flame. The fire fell back.
Low in the night sky flew Terra
Two. It had grown since it floated
upward from the saddle shelf a few
hours earlier.

The Troubadour smiled. "In only
three hours comes the midnight of
this planet. Terra One will die!
But even as it falls the sky will be
filled with the growing hope of
Terra Two. It is a world that you
will never enter, World Hater."

"You cannot kill me, nor control
me. I go to any world I wish. I once
brought civil war to Lifeland itself.
Have you forgotten?" The Prince
of Mirrors sneered at the world
growing above the flames.

Invictrix soared abruptly back
through the flames and settled
suddenly. Surprised, the Dark Prince
stumbled backward and fell
ingloriously to the charred ground.
He looked up at Ansond who trailed
a long chain of heavy links.

Light-Raider pawed the earth and
it opened in an awesome rift. From
the great scar the Hater could hear
the moaning from the Canyon of the
Damned.

"No . . . no!" cried the World Hater.

The Singer leapt from Light-Raider. The ancient struggle began again in fury. Hate tore at Love for the remaining hours. Terra Two loomed larger and larger until it filled the sky. Close to midnight, the World Hater in desperation flung his sword at the Troubadour.

The Golden Knight now entered into the struggle. He grasped the discarded sword and wielded it to split away the Hater's torn and dented armor.

Evil stood naked.

Ansond knew he could not put an end to the evil prince with the sword, for they had both been made to live forever. So he took the chain and wound it round the Hater's wounded body.

The Hater cursed the Singer and his Golden Knight and poured his scorn on Terra Two.

Dreamer beheld the final moments of the ancient struggle. The World Hater would live forever but never move again. He would hate but never enter Terra Two.

Invictrix nudged him toward the great rift. Over and over he rolled.

At the edge of the crevasse Invictrix
nudged him one more time. He
tumbled into the abyss and
plummeted away.

The ground closed.

Dreamer followed Ansond and the
Troubadour back to the waiting
army. The soldiers like himself
were all unharmed.

The War of Fire was over.

The Singer led the Army of Liberation
back upon the skyway.

At midnight the two worlds collided.
Terra one split away and then
dissolved. Terra Two rolled on in
youth.

XXIV

An old astronomer clasped his
    protégé and said,
"If Polaris dies tonight,
Be assured some greater light
Will take its place."

Ansond guided his mount above
a mountain range. He saw the
spires of the City of the Troubadour.
A lovely city without walls, for
walls though not forbidden were
forgotten. In worlds where evil has
not come walls never come to mind.

Invictrix skimmed a sunlit tower
and flew down to the plaza where
the children played. The steed
alighted. Ansond walked through
an arched portal and saw the Singer
sitting with his lyre. He saw
Ansond and rose to meet him.

The two embraced.

"Earthmaker is sovereign love!"
said Ansond.

"The music of the universe!" agreed
the Troubadour.

"Halana to the Father-Spirit!"
cried the Golden Knight.

"Come with me!" the Singer said.

They walked to the Plaza of Peace.
In the center of the square a
sphere of bright transparent glass
rested on one crystal's very point.

In the center of the sphere was a
world about the size that Terra Two

had been the day she rode into the
final battle of the War of Fire.

"It is Terra One—a replica,
exact and scaled," the Singer said.

"Forever sealed?" inquired Ansond.

"Forever," agreed the Troubadour.

"And we can never hear the anguish
from its center?" The Golden
Knight seemed troubled.

"Never. There shall be silence
where the Dark Prince writhes in
chains."

"He is small indeed to live in such
a tiny world as this."

"His is a dwindling point of death
within a growing universe of joy."

"Come," said the Singer. They
walked again.

Soon they came to a grand reliquary
on a distant ivory causeway. There
was a cube of glass and deep within
a replica of the Great Machine of
Death.

"Why keep this?" Ansond asked.

"It was the only hope of Terra One.
Those who walk this newer world are
here because I chose to die down
there between the gears and ropes."

"What was it like to die?" the
Golden Knight asked.

"Be grateful you shall never have
to know."

The Troubadour looked thoughtfully
away. "When it was over, I held
a new relationship with men. Even
Terra One died. Death does not
matter." The Singer gestured to
the glistening world of Terra
Two. "Dying is not final, only life."

Ansond looked at the scars of death
still marking the Prince's hands.

"You are the Singer, Prince and
Troubadour!"

There was music all around them in
the air.

They sang the Star-Song, and far
above the Crystal Chair, their
music drifted outward on the
universe.

"Earthmaker viewed the sculptured
    dignity
Of man, God-like and strident,
    President
Of everything that is,
    content to be
His intimate and only earthen
    friend."

HALANA.

THE FINALE

a poetic narrative in the tradition of C. S. Lewis's Narnia Chronicles and J. R. R. Tolkien's Lord of the Rings trilogy—is Calvin Miller's completion to his own trilogy which includes the very popular *The Singer* and *The Song*. In this final volume, Miller tells the story of the Singer's last battle with World Hater and envisions in dynamic prose-poetry the winding up of history on Terra One and the creation of Terra Two. As *The Singer* parallels the story of the Gospels and *The Song* parallels the book of Acts, so *The Finale* is an artistic retelling of the Book of Revelation. All three books are now available in a boxed set.

Calvin Miller is a graduate of Oklahoma Baptist University and holds the Doctor of Ministries degree from Midwestern Baptist Seminary. He is currently a pastor in Omaha, Nebraska, and is the author of *Once Upon a Tree, Poems of Protest and Faith, Sixteen Days on a Church Calendar, Burning Bushes and Moon Walks, A Thirst for Meaning, That Elusive Thing Called Joy, Transcendental Hesitation* and *A View from the Fields.*

The cover and interior illustrations are by Joe DeVelasco, a Chicago artist whose innovative work has appeared in many books and magazines.

The Finale is set in 10 point Palatino roman and printed by the R. R. Donnelley & Sons Co., The Lakeside Press, Chicago, Illinois, and Crawfordsville, Indiana. The cover is printed by Frank Prasil Graphics, Evanston, Illinois.